Natural Treasures of Northeast Florida by Beverly J. Fleming

I0119144

Natural Treasures of Northeast Florida by Beverly J. Fleming

A Guide to National Treasures of Northeast Florida
Beverly J. Fleming

ISBN-13: 978-0-9990882-4-1

First Edition published July 1, 2000
Second Edition published August 29, 2019

A Guide to

Natural Treasures of Northeast Florida

by

Beverly J. Fleming

Dedication

This book is dedicated in loving memory to my grandfather, John Dow Millsap. My first lessons in nature were received from him.

Acknowledgments

My grateful appreciation goes to my many teachers throughout the years. Also to those who have helped put this book together: Toni W. Crawford, June Weltman, Roger Bass and Gail Compton. Thank you to Eileen King for the use of her beautiful Limpkin photograph on the cover of this book. And to my husband, Dale, for his long suffering patience with my hours spent on the computer.

Photo Credits

Limpkin photo by Eileen King
All others by Beverly Fleming, author

Table of Contents

Introduction

Living along the St. Johns River for more than 15 years was a wonderful experience. The part of the river we got to know well was located between Kendall Creek and Kentucky Branch. Hollowes Cove, one of the river's best fish hatcheries, is located in that area.

Our experiences with fishing and boating, the daily changes of weather on the water and the vast array of natural neighbors such as limpkin, otter, bobcat, eagles and ospreys, fox, deer, turkey, turtles, alligators and other animals too numerous to mention provided us daily lessons and a lifetime of treasured memories.

This workbook was designed to help those who have not had such an experience to become better acquainted with the natural treasures of the NE Florida area. By becoming more familiar with these treasures we can become more appreciative of their values.

The Learning Process

Learning about the natural characteristics of the area you inhabit is a lot like the process a child undergoes as it matures. We can set ourselves on that road to learning by first taking tiny baby steps. Getting started is key to learning about our place on the planet.

Tiny babies know almost nothing about the world around them, yet they can recognize their mother's heart beat and voice. They are sensitive to hot and cold, to loud sounds and to the soft crooning of lullabies.

As time passes, they begin to show preferences for colors. They feel safe in their own rooms. At a more advanced age, they explore the whole house, learning where sharp corners are located and where the rug will trip them. In a few more years they will be outside, exploring their blocks and getting to know the neighbors.

This is when children are the most ambitious to learn all the answers to what, where, when, why and how. They ask a million questions and aren't content until they have explored every subject.

When they go to school, they find many new things to learn. Often, this is where a turning point takes place. They begin to become familiar with television, computers, electronic games and much more. Often, in their exuberance to learn all these things, they forget about the fun of learning about nature and the great outdoors.

They may not get the opportunity to make their own entertainment among the fields and grasses or the leaves and woods. Streams and mountains go unseen, birds are unheard, flowers unsmelled, fuzzy catkins are unfelt and sweet berries untasted. The natural wonders available are viewed only on the television screen.

Often, this is why some of us grow up knowing nothing about our own back yards. We may have seen all the wonders of the world without leaving the couch but we haven't a clue as to where our local food is grown or what the next phase of the moon will be.

With the help of this little booklet, maybe we can begin to take some tiny baby steps to learn more about the area we live in. We need to know what kind of soil we live on and where our water comes from.

If we try, we can learn to identify an eagle from an osprey, a monarch butterfly from a viceroy butterfly, a green-eyed daisy from blue-eyed grass. We can learn to hear the wind through pines and crickets in the grass. Frogs will croak and birds will sing and we will know them by their voices.

We can feel the smooth bark of a wild cherry tree or the rough-textured bark of an oak. And as we learn to tell the differences, we will also learn bout the sameness of each thing in our universe. Are the grains of sand in our back yard related to the rocks along the Appalachian Trail? How is that connection made?

As we learn about our bio region, we can expect to become more aware of the connections between the things in our immediate area and the things in other areas. We will be able to compare the laws of nature to the laws of our land. We may find ways of relating to plants and animals we never thought of before.

And after we have learned more about our own region, we may also be better able to understand the web of connections among all living things, not only in our own area, but in all areas. The things we do to each other are the very things we do to ourselves in the long run. As we become more comfortable with our awareness, we may find ways of changing our behavior to better reflect how we can live in harmony with other living things of the world.

Beverly J. Fleming
St. Augustine, Florida
July 1, 2000

Ask Yourself These Questions

How can we care about something we know little about? If we are not aware of the natural world around us, how can we live in harmony with it?

The following is a fun way to rate your knowledge of your own area.

1. In your own back yard or common yard of your apartment, how many trees do you know by name?
2. Can you name ten species of birds that feed in your yard?
3. What are they eating?
4. Of that ten species, can you name which are resident year round and which are migratory?
5. Can you name ten species of wild flowers you pass on your way to work?
6. Name six kinds of fish in the nearest large body of water.
7. Can you name five native edible plants of your region?
8. In what season would you find them?
9. Name three endangered plant species that inhabit your area.
11. Name three poisonous plants of your region.
11. Can you describe the life cycle of a butterfly?
12. Name five butterflies in your area.
13. Do you know how many species of poisonous snakes live in your state?
14. Do all of them inhabit your region?

Now grade your self on how many correct answers you have.

Scoring:
0-4 correct-------How did you get this far in life?
5-8 correct-------There may be hope for you yet.
9-12 correct------You have a firm grip on reality.
13 or better-------Congratulations! Your place in the web of life is secure.

NOTES

Lament for the Limpkin

Living on the St. Johns River just outside Orangedale in Northwest St. Johns County was a dream come true for my husband and me. We lived on 5,436 acres of woodland property owned by St. Joe Paper Company. We were hired as land overseers. It was like living in a nature preserve.

Most of our duties consisted of watching for and reporting fires, checking to be sure the gates along State Road 13 were locked, watching for and reporting trespassers and assisting with the organization of a hunting club on the property. We lived and worked there for seventeen years.

This setting was comfortable for my husband and myself as we both grew up in rural areas. As a native Floridian my husband's knowledge related to the area. I learned about NE Florida after I moved here in the early seventies.

During the time we lived on the property, we learned about many of the plants and animals of that specific area. We boated and fished the river. We went on photography excursions so I could capture images of the natural habitats. We set up wildlife feeding stations. We studied the habits of the wild turkeys and the deer. We paid particular attention to the migration of birds. We fed the Canada geese when they stopped on the river during their migration. We observed the courtship and mating of eagles and owls. We listened to the bobcats calling at night beneath the bedroom window.

The wildlife soon accepted our intrusion. We matched our breakfast and dinner routine to their natural early morning and dusk feeding times. As long as we didn't make any very sudden moves, they would observe us through the kitchen window just as we observed them.

Wild tom turkeys strutted their stuff to mostly indifferent females in the dusty track of the driveway. Their pale blue heads and scarlet engorged wattles brightened as they encountered an encroaching male. Their tails fanned farther and the primaries of the wings dragged down leaving lines in the dust as the two squared off in a sparring match. The glossy bronze feathers of their breasts and the long straight white tipped feathers of the tails littered the yard during molting season. The mothers paraded their youngsters past the window to the feeding station as soon as they were a couple of weeks old.

On early morning trips through the pinewood flats, we often see the blue-purple blossoms of Bartram's Ixia. A lone patch of Lady Lupine was located on a sandy bank near the property boundary. The orange flare of Pine Lilies and fringed orchids could be seen during autumn. And no journey to the woods was complete without checking the American Bald Eagle nest in a huge pine tree near the upper edge of the property.

Gopher tortoise inhabit the woods. We see their yawning burrows and catch them grazing nearby. Box turtles patrolled the garden paths looking for a meal of snails, worms or other insects. Sliders and soft-shelled turtles come ashore to dig holes and lay eggs in the sand of the yard or driveway.

Deer browse the edges of the yard, occasionally lifting their graceful heads and flicking their ears to detect any changes. Small fawns frolicking around their mothers legs as she warily fed on the native grasses and shrubs we left standing. Although she seemed to have her mind on other things, her liquid brown eyes suddenly would be staring right as us if we so much as rose from our chairs.

Each year we remained, we learned more about the area. We learned about the butterflies and their host plants. Zebra Swallowtails lay eggs on the pawpaws with their brownish maroon flowers. Spicebush and Tiger Swallowtails flew among the Sassafras and bay trees. One of our greatest delights was to try to identify the many Hairstreak butterflies before they flew off.

We learned about Indian pipes and Column stinkhorn fungus. We walked the paths of partridgeberry through the century old, moss draped oak and hickory trees. The hatching of baby Wood ducks riveted us to our deck chairs as the tiny bundles plummeted from their nest cavity onto the duff at the base of the Cypress tree that was their home.

I photographed juvenile Yellow Crowned Night Herons. They are really wild looking birds at that stage. The fuzzy down that later becomes crests on their heads stands straight up like an unruly crew cut and their large staring eyes seem too big for their heads.

One of the most enjoyable observations was that of a Limpkin family that lived in the mouth of the nearby Kendall Creek. The plaintive wail of these secretive, large brown and white wading birds could be heard at night and on cloudy days. We watched them hunt for apple snails and delighted in finding a spot where they had taken several to open. The empty shells showed just how the luscious meat had been extracted.

The adult Limpkins built a nest on a floating island of vegetation and grass about twelve feet across and raised at least two clutches of youngsters there. Bur the year after we saw them on the platform, the Army Corps of Engineers came along and sprayed the area with herbicides. The Corp engineer said it was to keep the waters of the creek open to navigation. And the spray worked. The vegetation, including the floating grass island where the birds nested, died. So did the eggs of the apple snails.

The Limpkins moved away. The Canada geese stopped coming. The eel grass beds died and manatees no longer rolled their bulky gray bodies in the shallows near the dock. The black bass became harder to find. Shell crackers stopped bedding on the flats. The river, at least in that area, died.

We continued to live there a few more years but the river just wasn't the same. We missed hearing the honking of Canada geese on cool fall mornings. But most of all, we missed the plaintive voice of the mysterious Limpkin calling at night and on cloudy days. *Kree-ow, kree-ow, kree-ow.*

Since then I have seen Limpkins on the St. Johns River around Hountoon Island. Although the river is coming back to life in the Orangedale area, I have not seen Limpkins return to that area to nest. Hopefully conditions will continue to improve to the point where they will return in the near future.

© by Eileen King

Limpkin

NOTES

The Beginning Process

The story of the Limpkin illustrates just how intimately you can get to know a place. The Limpkin are gone but as the general attitude and actions of our communities change we hope to see their return.

Our actions affect the air, water, soil, our forests, wildlife, the birds, bees and butterflies. These are just some of the things we must begin to know. And then we must begin to understand their connection to each other and to us.

As we begin to understand that connection, we will hopefully develop an ethic or a system for determining correct action in relation to these elements. In other words, when we understand our place in the natural world, we can begin to make decisions based on that knowledge.

One thing that we must remember is that some features of our area change over time. Forests are cleared, developments take their place. A hurricane comes through and we lose some of the beach front, or a beach re-nourishment project takes place and some creature's home is covered up. Some species adapt to these and other kinds of changes and some don't.

Change such as growth, filling of wetlands, and removal of trees affect other things such as our water table. As more and more residents move into the area or prolonged drought strikes, we find we are faced with changes in our wells and in the depth of area lakes and ponds.

Beginning from the ground up, so to speak, we find that our region of Northeast Florida is made up of sandy soil with a limestone foundation. We have a variety of surface habitats such as wetlands and marshes, scrub, pine forest and woodlands, farm and range land, and dunes.

The "backbone" of the Northeast Florida area is a limestone ridge running from north to south in the Keystone area. This ridge is very near the surface and is a factor in that area being a major recharge area for the Floridan aquifer. Water, seeping into the ground along that ridge accumulates in underground chambers. Over extended periods of time this water gradually seeps east toward the ocean.

If you look at a map of Florida, you will be able to visualize an imaginary lateral line down through the center of the state. As the land rose from the ocean, the waters of the eastern half of the state flowed to the Atlantic and the waters of areas west of the center flowed toward the Gulf of Mexico. Obviously, the highest elevations in the state are on the north end while the south end, containing the Everglades, is barely above sea level.

Over time, various ridges of dunes formed as the land mass gradually rose from the sea to its highest elevation. The ridges were eventually covered with a wide variety of natural vegetation, including grasses, vines, shrubs and trees. Although the soil is relatively poor, farming and cattle ranching eventually became the major sources of income for the state until recently. Tourism is now the number one industry. And that industry may affect some of the area's natural resources in an adverse way.

Water, it's quality and quantity, affect all of us as well as the plants and animals that inhabit the same area. Therefore, whether we get the average 50 inches of rainfall per year, or more or less than that amount, it is to our advantage to protect and preserve it. Knowing about Florida's water resources makes us better able to make wise decisions.

"Recommended reading, *Florida's Water Resources* by Armalee Fegan, B.A."

NOTES

Trees

Trees still cover approximately one half of our state although more are being cut each day for our ever-expanding growth. We need their greeness even more than before to clean the air and water of the pollution that growth generates.

Trees clean the air by taking in carbons and putting oxygen back into the air. They clean the water by absorbing it. Then transpiration takes place, putting moisture back into the air. This moisture will eventually come down as rain.

Many native trees are grown in the home landscape along with ornamentals from other parts of the world. Below are some of those native species we see in our area of the state.

The Florida State Tree is **Sabal Palm** (Sabal palmetto), also called Cabbage Palm. It is a slow growing palm, reaching a height of 40 to 60 feet at maturity. The leaves or fans are glossy green above and gray green below. As the leaves die off, they are usually torn from the trunk by the wind, leaving "boots" on the trunk. As the trees get older, the boots are shed leaving the trunk smooth. The flowers, fragrant and greenish white, are produced in long clusters. The heart, or bud, at the top of the tree was eaten by early Florida Indians and later by the early settlers. Unfortunately, if you cut out the heart, the tree dies.

Most of the **Longleaf Pine** (Pinus palustris), or Southern Pines, have been cut in this portion of the state. Our only Longleaf Pine forests, located within the Apalachicola National Forest, are home to colonies of Red-cockaded Woodpeckers, a threatened species. **Loblolly Pine** (Pinus taeda) or **Slash Pine** (Pinus elliottii) is now more common here. Our earliest industries, shipbuilding and turpentining, and later paper making, relied heavily on pines.

Live Oak, (Quercus virginiana) is a popular tree because it lives for hundreds of years and stays green throughout the year. The leaves are egg shaped and are pushed aside as new ones form. This tree rarely grows to more than 60 feet in height, yet it can cover an area nearly three times that size. Live Oaks were also used in ship building.

The **Sugarberry** (Celtis laevigata) or **Hackberry** is a deciduous tree growing to 80 feet. It has a smooth grayish bark and many spreading branches. The Mourning Cloak butterfly lays its eggs on the light green leaves and a wide variety of wildlife feed on the ripe blue fruit. This tree, once established, is very drought tolerant.

The scarlet and yellow fall leaves of the **Florida Maple** (Acer saccharum floridanum) is almost as colorful as the paired, winged seeds, which come whirling off this tree in the spring. This is a fast growing tree used in new yards to give "instant" shade to the homeowner. It is a natural part of the hardwood forests of Northeast Florida.

The fragrant six to eight inch wide white flowers of the **Southern Magnolia** (Magnolia grandiflora) are legendary. This evergreen tree may reach 65 feet in height. It has smooth gray-brown bark on the trunk and large leathery dark green leaves with bronze undersides. Cone-like pods produce seeds resembling coffee beans to provide food for woodpeckers and other birds.

Trees provide shade, nesting sites for birds, homes for squirrels and other annuals, food for wildlife, flowers, and oxygen. They absorb water and transpire it into the air. Our dependence on trees is many-fold.

"Recommended reading, *Trees* by James Underwood Crockett and the Editors of Time Life Books."

Florida Maple

NOTES

Birds

You don't need to visit a birding hot spot to get an introduction to bird watching. It is something we all can do in our own backyard or neighborhood.

Birds are a natural indicator of the environment. When you are surrounded by a healthy, balanced environment, you will see a wide variety of birds.

One of the most common birds of our area is the **Carolina Wren** (Thryothorus ludovicianus), a small warm reddish brown bird with a conspicuous white eyebrow stripe. This wren ranges throughout the eastern United States and is comfortable in the city as well as the country. It can be seen flitting around garages, gardens and the shrubby areas of your yard.

This little bird is a prolific insect eater. It may raise as many as three clutches of babies each summer, depending on the weather. It often nests in hanging planters and is quite content to be around humans.

Since this bird is not a seed eater, it is not attracted to bird feeders. Put a bird bath in your yard or garden, however, and you are almost certain to see this species. It is not a high flyer, preferring to stay near the ground. It has a clear three-syllabled song, "*chirpity, chirpity, chirpity, chirp.*"

Another common bird of the area is the **Northern**

Cardinal (Cardinalis). The bright red male and brownish red female inhabit the eastern half of the United States and are expanding their range north and west. Both male and female birds have a crest.

Cardinals willingly come to feeders, preferring black oil sunflower seed and white millet. They love woodland edges and thickets and are equally at home in town or country. Their "cheery, cheery, cheer" call rings clear, especially in the early morning.

Both the Northern Cardinal and the Carolina Wren are year round residents of the Northeast Florida area.

The most gaudy colored bird of our area is the male **Painted Bunting** (Passerina ciris). He has a blue-violet head, a lime green back, red on the rump and underparts, and dark olive brown wings and tail. His drab mate, on the other hand, is greenish above blending to a greenish yellow below. She is our only all green finch type bird. Both are common at feeders and birdbaths.

The Painted Bunting is a migratory bird, arriving to raise young along coastal Florida beginning in late March to early April and leaving in the fall. Its preferred habitat is the woodland edge of your yard, and you will get see an avian acrobatic show every day as the young learn to clasp seed heads and ride them down to the nearest perch.

One of the most graceful birds to be seen in Northeast Florida is the **Swallow-tailed Kite** (Elanoides forficatus). This black and white bird of prey lives on large insects, reptiles and rodents. The Swallow-tailed Kite inhabits wooded river swamps during the summer months but leaves the United States for warmer climates in the winter.

This elegant bird is shaped like a large Barn Swallow with a deeply forked black tail, solid white head and underparts and mostly black wings. It soars and spirals, many times with partners, in the clear summer sky.

The **American Bald Eagle** (Haliaeetus leucocephalus) is one of our most notable success stories. Florida has the second largest breeding population, next to Alaska, of this once rare and endangered species. Its solid white head and tail and bright yellow beak with solid dark body helps distinguish this large bird of prey from the more common osprey or fish eagle.

Eagles prefer to nest in living trees while osprey often make their nests in dead trees along rivers, streams and cypress ponds. Both feed on fish, but the eagle also feeds on roadside kills. The courtship spirals of the breeding pairs can often be seen in late fall as they return to their nest sites to begin another nesting season.

Young eaglets usually hatch in late January or early February in this area. During March and April, the young are fed and finally fledge, or fly from the nest, by July and are able to join their parents in their summer travels. The young do not get their adult plumage until they are three or four years old, remaining mostly solid brown with some white until then.

If your yard contains a pond or small water feature with fish, you may become accustomed to seeing wading birds up close. Although some, such as the **Great Blue Heron** (Ardea herodias) are shy, solitary birds, others such as the **Little Blue Heron** (Florida caerulea) can become quite tolerant of humans and may even inhabit a favorite post near a fisherman in hopes of getting a free handout. Both feed on fish, reptiles, amphibians and insects.

The Great Blue Heron stands almost four feet high. It is our largest heron and inhabits all parts of North America. The upper parts of this bird are slate gray with light underparts, while breast and thighs are a rusty chestnut color. The dagger-like bill is bright yellow. The head is white with longer black feathers at the crest.

Little Blue Herons are approximately 22 inches long. The adult is predominately dark blue slate with a brownish head. The bill is blue with a dark tip and the legs are greenish yellow. The Little Blue Heron is more social than the Great Blue, often roosting with a group of its own kind in the shrubby growth along streams and rivers.

The Green Heron (Butorides striatus) is the smallest of our herons with a length of only 19 inches and a wingspan of only 25 inches. As indicated by the name, this bird has a green back as well as dark green on the wings, tail and head. The rest of the head and neck are reddish brown. The legs are short and bright yellow while the beak is long and greenish black. Only when this bird is alarmed or when it is striking at its prey can you tell the length of the neck. Usually, the head rests near the shoulders with the neck folded. This bird loves wooded areas and will stake out a feeding area around a pond, chasing away intruders with a loud squawk.

The endangered **Wood Stork** (Mycteria americana) is a large bird with a bare dark gray wrinkled head and upper neck. The white wings with black edges can span 66 inches. The rest of the body is white. A year round resident, the wood stork can often be seen feeding in deep roadside ditches and standing around on golf courses. It feeds mostly on fish but will also eat snakes, lizards, frogs, large insects and small mammals. Wood Storks nest in colonies high in tall trees. Loss of suitable nesting habitat has caused this species to decline to the point of being placed on the endangered species list.

The most showy of our native wading birds is the **Roseate Spoonbill** (Ajaia ajaia). Mainly because plume hunters slaughtered them by the thousands, they were almost wiped out in Florida. However, strict enforcement of laws have given them time to recuperate, although they are still a species of special concern. Body plumage on these birds ranges from rosy gray to deep pink depending on the age of the bird and the season. The spoon-shaped bill is an identifying feature. During the mating period, a yellow crown appears on the yellowish green featherless head. Legs are a deep rosy red. Young birds are fed by regurgitation of small fish, insects, crustaceans, mollusks and some aquatic vegetation.

"To learn more about birds, books such as *A Field Guide to the Birds* by Roger Tory Peterson or *Guide to Florida Wading Birds* by Robert Anderson are helpful."

Wood Storks

Wild Flowers

Wild flowers grow anywhere and everywhere in North Florida. A crack in the sidewalk will often sport the yellow blossoms of **Wood Sorrel** (Oxalis stricta) while even the driest roadside will be covered by the red and yellow pinwheels of **Blanket Flower** (Gaillardia pulchella). Bluish-purple to pale **Florida Violets** (Viola floridana) grow in many shady suburban yards. Red spires of **Coralbean** (Erythina herbacca) line the roadside along the beach.

Florida has a dazzling array of native wildflowers, species that grew here before European influence. But there are also many wildflowers that were brought here, intentionally or otherwise, from far away places. We have European settlers to thank for the **Common Dandelion** (Taraxacum officinale) and **White Sweet Clover** (Melilotus alba). **Hairy Indigo** (Indigofera hirsuta) comes from Africa and **Creeping Oxeye** (Wedelia trilobata) from the West Indies. These and other new comers are all established now, sometimes crowding out true native species.

Loss of habitat due to growth has made others more scarce. Changing land practices such as clear cutting, controlling natural fires and changes in weather patterns have caused others to become less common. Many have yet to be studied and others have yet to be identified.

Each has a place in our system and we must save a place for each.

Florida, Land of Flowers. With such an incredible collection, it is hard to decide which is the best time of year for wildflowers. Because of the relatively mild climate here, each season has some very special blossoms, making trips to open fields, woodlands, swamps and river banks a joy.

Each person can get to recognize his or her favorites as they go to and from work and their other daily activities. Driving through the city streets, you get an opportunity to study disturbed sites and the plants that grow there. If you live in a suburb, the daily drive might take you past wetlands, sand hills or pine flatwoods. Each of these areas offer their seasonal beauty to those who are interested. And for those who live in the country, the array is an almost endless succession of grace and beauty.

Easy to identify flowers such as morning glory come in many varieties in our area. Rose-purple **Glades Morning-glory** (Ipomoea Sagittata) grows in wet areas, often near the coast while the variety with purple flowers (Ipomoea indica) bloom in thickets and disturbed sites. **Blue Spiderwort** (Tradescantia ohiensis) flowers greet you in your morning travels but their buds are tightly closed during the afternoon commute.

Wild Azaleas (Rhododendron canescens) perfume the woods in the early spring while the huge white blossoms of **Moonflowers** (Ipomoea alba) scent the night air. We have several varieties of rare and unusual flowers. It is a treat to be able to take people to see such unusual flowers as the **Yellow Fringed Orchid** (Platanthera cilaris) or **Lady Lupine** (Lupinus villosus). **Grass Pink Orchids** (Calopogon tuberosus) seem to be rarer now and you will seldom see **Blue Curls** (Trichostema dichotomum) unless you know just where to look for them.

Just as early explorers were impressed with the wide diversity of flowering plants, new residents are often overwhelmed by the many new semi-tropical varieties growing in our yards and gardens. Some of these are native species while many are imports of other lands. Approximately 300 species of native wildflowers have been identified as endemic according to Walter Kingsley in his book *The Guide to Florida Wildflowers*. And Bell and Taylor in their *Florida Wild Flowers and Roadside Plants* also help us identify the incredible number of colorful species we encounter on our daily excursions.

Since most of us are not botanists, it is good to be able to recognize some structural characteristics of flowers in order to identify them. Note the leaf shape, color of the petals, height of the plant, and the habitat where it is growing. Are the flowers solitary or do they grow in clusters? Is there fruit on the plant? Does it grow in the sun or shade? These clues will help to identify most wildflowers in our state.

One of the earliest of the spring wildflowers is **Yellow Jessamine** (Gelsemium sempervirens), a woody vine with bright yellow trumpet-shaped fragrant flowers. These hardy vines often grow to the tops of roadside trees and shrubs, cascading in graceful falls of blossoms for long periods of time. Although somewhat invasive in disturbed areas, these plants make a good climbing plant for a trellis or arbor in the home landscape.

The violet blue blossoms of the **Flag Iris** or **Prairie Iris** (Iris hexagona) can also be seen in the spring in area roadside ditches and other low ground. They have light green sword-shaped leaves growing in fans and can grow to three feet tall. They can be seen growing along the St. Johns River and are a good source of early nectar for Ruby Throated Hummingbirds.

The **Hooded Pitcherplant** (Sarracenia minor) is another spring flowering native of moist roadsides, wet pinelands and marshes. This insectivorous plant absorbs nutrients from insects digested in the water filled hollow tubular leaves. Each leaf has downward pointing hairs on the inside to keep ants and other insects from escaping. The lemony yellow flowers are often hard to spot because of their downward facing stance.

Late spring and summer bring on the **Trumpet** or **Coral Honeysuckle** (Lonicera sempervirens) for hungry hummingbirds. This vine-like shrub is common along old fences in central and north Florida. The trailing stems hold clusters of bright red trumpet shaped flowers and deep green leaves.

Lavender spikes of **Horsemint** or **Spotted Beebalm** (Monarda punctata) grow along sandy disturbed sites in central and north Florida. Their flowers and more noticeable darker upper bracts appear during late spring, summer and into fall. This square stemmed plant is only one of many wild mints in the area.

You have to be outside early to see the beautiful blue flowers of **Spiderwort** (Tradescantia osiensis) as they close soon after the sun hits them. This member of the dayflower family blooms all year throughout the state and can be found along moist roadsides and meadows. It is often cultivated in lawns as it is one of the few true blue flowers to be found here.

Another recognizable roadside beauty is the **Blackeyed Susan** (Rudbeckia hirta). The bright to dark yellow ray florets encircle the dark brown raised disk florets at the center of this common blossom. Found throughout the state and blooming almost the entire year, clusters of this plant are easy to spot along roadsides on the way to work.

The **Lance-leaved Coreopsis** (Coreopsis lanceolata) is the state flower of Florida. It is a member of the aster or daisy family. The blossoms of this plant are formed of yellow disk florets as well as yellow ray florets. The Department of Transportation plants giant swaths of these flowers along the roadways in north Florida, as they make a great welcoming statement to those entering the state.

In the fall and winter, the pinelands are filled with spikes of **Deer-tongue** (Carphephorus paniculatus) and **Vanilla Plant** (Carphephorus odoratissima). Both are members of the aster family and both are purple. The stems of Deer-tongue are hairy and the lower heads are more spike like than the flatter heads of the Vanilla Plant. As its name implies, this plant has a distinct vanilla odor, especially when dried.

Ditches, wet grounds and swamps throughout the state are filled with Fall Aster (Aster elliottii) throughout fall and into early winter. The easy-to-identify flower heads are a showy purple with yellow-red centers. Plants are usually around three feet tall but may get much higher along stream banks.

Although these are only a few of the many exciting species to be seen along Florida's roadsides, they are among the easiest to spot as commuters go to and from the workplace each day. To find out more about our wildflowers, join a garden club, take a wildflower walk with a park ranger or search the library shelves for wildflower books.

For more information on wildflowers read *Florida Wildflowers and Roadside Plants* by Bell and Taylor.

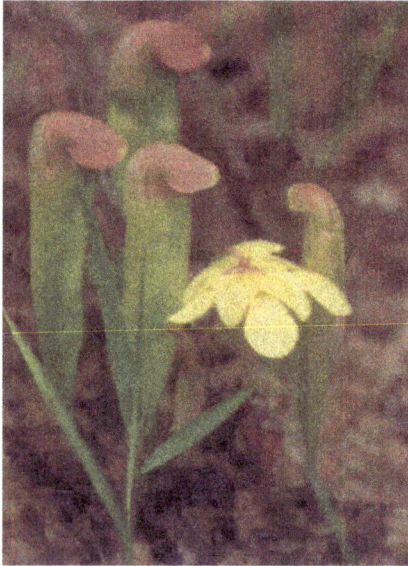

Hooded Pitcher Plant

Fish

Fish inhabit almost every body of water in our area, including tiny ditches located beside the road. If you live near the ocean, chances are you will know more about saltwater fish. If you live near the river, fresh water fish may be more familiar to you. But even if you aren't near a large body of water, fish can be found in small retention ponds or common lakes in development.

How did the fish get there? Were they stocked by man or was nature the contributor?

One way fish are moved by nature is when flooding occurs. At this time, they move from rivers and other large bodies of water into adjoining ditches and swamps. The Mosquito Fish (Gambusia affinis) is one of the small species able to live in very shallow ditches and swamps. They can do this because they can survive low levels of oxygen, sometimes even gulping air if necessary.

Large mouth **Black Bass**, **Red Eared Sunfish**, **Warmouth Perch**, and **Copperhead** are some of the fresh water fish we are familiar with in the St. Johns River. **Red Bass**, **flounder** and **drum** are found in the Intracoastal Waterway. **Whiting** are seen in the surf, and off shore there are **Kingfish**, **Wahoo** and **dolphin** just to name a few.

Each fish inhabits a different area of the water, seeking its own level and feeding habitat. Each is able to swim into different environments and return to its own area. Each has a place to spawn and the tiny hatchlings move about to different areas as they grow and mature. Often one species preys upon another, yet this completes the interconnected aquatic web within the larger web of life.

Man's impact on this habitat results from over fishing some species, from contaminating the water from dredging, and from many other sources of irresponsible behavior.

When we fill in swamps, when we change the course of a waterway, when we cut canals across the country we impact habitat. When we pump huge amounts of water from the river or dump wastewater back into that river, we negatively impact the lives of fish and all other animals in the chain that depend on them.

Our fish eating birds include pelicans, heron, egrets, eagle, osprey and several other species. These birds would not be able to raise their young if they could not get fish to eat.

Some fish are indicator species for the quality of water. If the water is healthy, the fish appear healthy. But if the water is polluted, fish begin to show up with sores on their bodies or fish kills become more common. And when living creatures in the water become unhealthy, birds and other mammals that live on them cannot survive.

In the St. Johns River sport fishing is very popular. People often move here just for the fishing. Because some species have become somewhat depleted, may fisherman now practice catch and release methods, However, for some, fishing is done as a source of food. It is imperative that the quality of the river be kept to its highest standard so there will be healthy fish to eat.

Mullet and **catfish** are two common species which are popular for both recreation fishing and food. Many rural families living along the St. Johns River have been raised on fish, grits and hushpuppies.

Shad

NOTES

Weeds as Edible Plants

Ralph Waldo Emerson said "A weed is a plant whose virtues are not yet known to us."

However, many of our so-called weeds do have virtues as edible plants, medicinal plants, as basis for herbal teas, jellies and for use in cosmetics. And incredibly, these plants can even be found in city yards.

First and foremost, a word of warning. Always know the exact identity of a plant before you consider eating it. Also, be sure you collect plants from areas that are not contaminated by spraying. The third warning would be to try a small amount of a new plant to find out if you have any allergic reaction to it. We all have some food allergies and this seems to hold true for wild edibles as well.

Native plants, those that grow wild in the region before Europeans "discovered" America, were used by the native people who populated the area in their every day existence. **Coonti** (Zamia floridana) is an example. The root was pounded into a flour like substance to be used in cooking stews. Beware of the seeds of this plant, however as they are poison.

Cattail (Typha domingensis) is a common plant of ditches, ponds and other wet places, not only in our area, but throughout much of the United States. You can eat the bottom part of new shoots in spring time, add the pollen to bread dough or pancake batter or boil the new flowers and eat them as a cooked vegetable.

Our Florida state tree, the **Sabal Palm** (Sabal palmetto), or **Cabbage Palm** was a survival food for many Florida crackers. These were the people who first settled Florida to raise cattle on the vast grass lands. The term "cracker" is thought to have come from the cracking of the cowboys' whips. Swamp cabbage, the edible heart of the palm, was served up on many tables as it was easy to harvest on the long cattle drives. Harvesting the heart of the palm kills the tree, however.

Saw Palmetto (Serenoa repens) is often confused with young Sabal palms. The heart of the saw palmetto can be eaten just like the heart of the Sabal and the plant will not die. In addition, the palmetto fruits were also eaten by the American Indian. These fruits have been tested for their medicinal properties as well.

Many plants are well known for making tea. **Yaupon Holly** (Ilex vomitoria) was used by the American Indians to make a black tea used as a purgative. The reddish fruits of the **Shining Sumac** (Rhus copallina) and **Staghorn Sumac** (Rhus typhina) were used to make a drink similar to lemonade. **Sassafras** tea was a favorite drink of the early inhabitants and is still a popular tea. The leaves of the Sassafras albidum are used, dried and powdered, as an herb for flavoring Cajun dishes. It is called "file." Rose hips make another healthful tea. The hips are high in vitamin C.

In spring, look for small, new leaves of several edible greens for a fresh tasting salad. Young leaves of **Dollar Weed** or **Pennywort** (hydrocotyle umbellata), **Dandelion** (Taraxacum officinale), **Hawkweed** (Hieracium aurantiacum), **Lamb's Quarter** (Dhenopodium album) and **Oxalis** (Oxalis spp.) will combine to make a delicious salad as well as freeing you of many of the "weeds" you want to remove from your yard.

Wild Cherry (Prunus serotina), **Elderberry** (Sambucus simpsonii), **Prickly Pear cactus** (Opuntia spp.), **Pindo Palm** (Butia capitata) and **Blueberry** (Vaccinium spp.) all have delicious fruit which may be eaten raw, made into jellies or jams, used in baking or made into delicious wines.

And, of course, there are the blossoms of such beauties as the **Violet** (Viola floridana), **White Clover** (Trifolium repens), and **Spanish Needle** (Bidens pilosa) which are edible and nutritious.

These are just a few of the edible plants or weeds to be found in your area but once you get started on identifying and tasting these nutritious edibles you will want to continue to expand your knowledge and your menu.

Recommended reading: *I Eat Weeds* by Priscilla G. Bowers, a local author, or *A Field Guide to Edible Wild Plants* by Lee Peterson.

Sumac

Endangered Plants

Nancy C. Coile in her recent book, *Notes on Florida: Endangered and Threatened Plants*, mentions there are more than 500 native plants in Florida currently listed as either Endangered or Threatened. The Northeast Florida area has almost 50 species on the two lists. There are also six species of natives of this area on the list of Commercially Exploited Plants. Commercially exploited plants are those harvested from the wild and sold to the public.

The Regulated Plant Index is based on information provided by the Endangered Plant Advisory Council (EPAC), a group of seven individuals who represent academic, industry and environmental interests. Permits are sometimes given but penalties are also given to people who violate the laws regulating the destruction of these plants.

It would be difficult to describe many of the listed plants, as most people never see them. Visitors to the beach are always made aware of the endangered status of **Sea Oats** (Uniola paniculata). This is probably the most recognizable protected plant in Florida.

As a photographer, I have often searched our area for endangered plants to photograph. I am always careful not to disturb the site or the plants and seldom divulge their location unless it is to another very trusted photographer.

Bartram's Ixia (Sphenostigma coilestinum) is an endangered perennial, which grows from a bulb-like corm. It has one to three basil leaves, one or two stems, and one or two flowers. The petals are a blue-violet color, which is very hard to photograph. It has three petals and three petal-like sepals.

The plant grows in wet flatwoods, and wet prairies in Northeast Florida and blooms from April to June. You seldom see the flowers after 10 a.m. as they disappear when the sun hits them.

The next few plants are on the threatened list. The **Catesby** or **Pine Lily** (Lilium catesbaei) is a perennial herb of wet flatwoods and bogs. The leaves are alternate and linear. The flowers are orange-pink with darker freckles. The petals are clawed and recurved. It blooms in late August or early September.

Cardinal Flower (Lobelia cardinalis) is another perennial herb of riverbanks, springs and coastal hammocks. This is a bright red flower generally blooming in the fall.

Yellow-fringed Orchid (Platanthera ciliaris) also goes by the common name of orange plume. If you ever spot this terrestrial orchid you will immediately know how it got its common names. The many flowers, held high on a spike, are a butterscotch orange color with a fringed lip. They bloom at almost the same time as the Cateby Lilies and are found in bogs, swamps, marshes, pine savannas, flatwoods and flood plain forests in our area.

Another threatened perennial herb is the **Hooded**

Pitcher Plant (Sarracenia minor). The leaves of this plant are erect. The green pitcher turns reddish on the top if it is in full sun. The hood of this plant arches over the mouth. The petals of the flowers are yellow and hang with their faces down. Secretions inside the hood attract insects, which are then trapped and digested by the plant. This plant is found in ditches, bogs and pinelands.

On the Commercially Exploited list are **Wild Pink Azalea** (Rhododendron canescens) and **Coontie** (Zamia integrifolia) and both natives are available at many nurseries. However, those for sale have been grown for that purpose instead of being gathered from the wild as they once were. State law protects some endangered plants while Federal or other laws protect others.

Yellow Fringed Orchid

NOTES

Poisonous Plants

Many of the plants we come across in our daily routine are poisonous. The whole plant may be toxic or just one part, such as the seeds or the leaves, may cause a reaction.

Most people who have grown up in the county have had at least one experience with **Poison Ivy** or **Poison Oak**. But those who are city dwellers should be aware of the many plants around their house or apartment that may produce the same results or worse.

Common landscaping plants and houseplants may have one or more parts that are poisonous. Therefore, when we choose plants for landscaping or to grow in pots or planters, we should consider their toxicity as well as the beauty of their blossoms and foliage.

In our area, **Oleander** is one of the most common flowering shrubs planted in common areas such as along roadsides and along property lines. The leaves and branches of oleander are extremely poisonous. Eating only a few leaves may cause death in children or pose a danger to pets.

We all admire the beautiful red color of the festive **Poinsettia** during the winter holidays. Would we be so quick to bring it into our homes if we knew that only one leaf, if eaten by a child, could be deadly? Even the **Wild Poinsettia** (Euphorbia heterophylla), which is common in many yards and gardens of the area, is poisonous.

The romantic and graceful clusters of lavender or white **Wisteria** are common in southern gardens. These vines often grace arbors and pergolas in our area. In other parts of the state, they have taken over abandoned fences and even climbed to the top of pines, covering them completely. The seeds and pods of this plant are poison and if eaten, mild to severe digestive upset may occur.

Many gardeners in our area would feel highly deprived if they were not able to plant **azaleas** in their yards. The blossoms of these woody shrubs bloom profusely during the spring and add beauty wherever they are grown. But we should be aware that all parts of this plant are poisonous, and can be fatal if eaten.

The beautiful and fragrant **Narcissus** is a plant often grown in pots indoors. The bulbs of this plant are often forced so the blooms may be used as a decorative accent on the table. Most hostesses are not aware of the toxic qualities of those very bulbs, If eaten, they could cause nausea, vomiting, diarrhea, and could even be fatal.

Dieffenbachia and **Crown of Thorns**, two other common houseplants, are also toxic if eaten.

These are just a few of the more common plants we come into contact with daily. For information, ask for Bulletin number 175D, ***Poisonous Plants Around the Home***, by Erdman West. This bulletin can be obtained from University of Florida, Cooperative Extension Service, Institute of Food and Agricultural Sciences.

Wild Azalea

NOTES

Butterflies

Butterflies are another indicator species of the health of the environment because they not only inhabit the country but reside in the city as well. Wherever their basic requirements are met, you will find these fragile flying wonders among the plants and grasses. They are by far the most popular insects in the world, according to Jaret C. Daniels in his **Butterfly Gardening** book.

In addition to providing hours of pleasure for butterfly enthusiasts, butterflies are also major pollinators, spreading pollen over a wide range of native and cultivated plants. The adults and their larvae also provide food for birds, lizards, spiders, small mammals and other insects.

Our most well known butterfly is probably the **Monarch** (Danaus plexippus). Its beautiful orange wings with black veins and margins sprinkled with tiny white dots are seen throughout the state of Florida in sunny, open area such as fields, meadows, pastures and roadsides. The yellow, black and white larvae devour milkweed of various kinds including Asclepias incarnata, A. curassavica, and A. tuberosa.

The **Zebra Longwing** (Heliconius charitonius) is the Florida state butterfly. This butterfly is present year round in all of Florida where there are no hard freezes. They are seen most often in woodlands, forest edges and in yards where their favorite plant, the passionflower, is grown. The creamy white caterpillars with long black hairs feed on various native and exotic passionflower vines, including the maypop (Passiflora incarnata).

Common to open, sunny, moist areas such as roadside ditches is the **White Peacock Butterfly** (Anartia jatrophae). The prolific Frog Fruit (Phyla nodiflora), Ruellia (Ruellia occidentalis) and Smooth Water Hyssop (Bacopa mobbieri) are favorites of this pale beauty. They are a photographer's delight as they often sit for long periods in the sun with open wings.

Because of the wide variety of host plants it recognizes, the **Cloudless Sulphur** (Phoebus sennae) is probably the most often seen. Its pale yellow wings can be seen throughout Florida all year long. The female lays eggs on Partridge Pea (Cassia fasciculata), on Sickle-pod Senna (Cassia obtusifolia) and sensitive pea (Cassia nictitans) just to name a few of the host plants. You often see these butterflies sipping nectar from the purple flowers of Tall Verbena (Verbena bonariensis) or red Pentas (Pentas lanceolata).

One of the most easily identifiable larvae of any butterfly of Florida is that of the **Gulf Fritillary** (Agraulis vanillae). Because of its bright orange color and black spiky look, the caterpillar is easily seen on the green leaves of the passion vines it shares with the Zebra Longwing. The adults are mostly orange with a silvery iridescence to the underside of the hind wings. This butterfly is common in all parts of the state where there are no hard freezes. It inhabits sunny open pastures, roadsides and old fields.

There are four stages to a butterfly's life. The egg, larvae, pupa and adult are all identifiable in each species. Each egg is marked differently and is laid either singly or in clusters on a host plant. The larvae molt many times as they eat and grow larger. In the final stage their molt reveals a pupa or chrysalis. Just as each egg and caterpillar is distinct, so is the pupa. Within this casing, the butterfly forms.

It is very easy to entice butterflies to inhabit your yard and garden by supplying their basic needs. Plant nectar sources and host plants in both sun and shade if available. Pick a place out of the wind for your garden and plant in groupings. Be sure to provide plants for each season as many of the butterflies are active year round. Plant native species when possible. Provide a source of water such as a shallow dish with wet sand. A nice dark rock for basking in the sun is also a good addition to the garden.

Tiger Swallowtail

NOTES

Snakes

The very mention of the word "snake" is enough to bring shudders from many people, yet the number of poisonous snakes in Florida is few. The amount of good that snakes do for us far out weighs the bad. Snakes help to keep the rodent population in check, a vital aspect of ecology.

Of the 40 species of snakes in Florida, only six are poisonous and only five of those snakes are located in Northeast Florida.

Diamondback Rattlesnakes, **Canebrake Rattlesnakes** and **Pygmy Rattlesnakes** are all pit vipers with rattles at the end of their tails. The **Cottonmouth Moccasin** is a pit viper without rattles. All four of these snakes have fangs. They also all have elliptical or oval shaped eyes with a slit-like pupil.

The **Coral Snake** has small, hooked teeth, a round shaped eye with a round pupil.

There are two characteristics that can help people to distinguish poisonous snakes from non-poisonous snakes, according to a leading snakebite expert. Maynard Cox, a Jacksonville resident, is recognized worldwide as an authority on snakebites.

Except for the Coral snake, poisonous snakes have triangular-shaped heads while non-poisonous snakes have rounded heads. But Cox recommends looking at the tail instead of the head. Poisonous snakes have short, stubby tails while the tails of non-poisonous snakes are long, skinny and whip-like.

Cox says that contrary to popular belief, snakes are not aggressive. He believes the only time a snake will bite a human is if the snake is hurt, mad, cornered or scared. If you see a poisonous snake, turn and run away. The snake will not pursue you.

Cox also says that about ninety percent of snakebites occur on the extremities. About two thirds of the bites occur on the feet and legs and one third on the hands and arms. He says snakebites most often occur when a person accidently steps on a snake, reaches into an area where they can't see, or when they try to catch a snake.

Non-poisonous snakes include Southern Black Racer, Eastern Garter Snake, Red Rat Snake (corn snakes), Yellow Rat Snake, Eastern Hognose Snake, and Florida Water Snake. Your chances of coming across a non-poisonous snake are about 18 times greater than that of coming across a poisonous snake.

Poisonous snakes bite approximately 8,000 people in the United States each year. If bitten, proper treatment is essential. Do not cut, suck or apply a tourniquet to the bite.

Go immediately to the nearest emergency room or hospital and have someone call Maynard Cox at (904) 264-6512 at Clay County Sheriff's Office. He is on call 24 hours a day. He will see that you are properly treated for the bite you have received. Do not try to bring the snake with you.

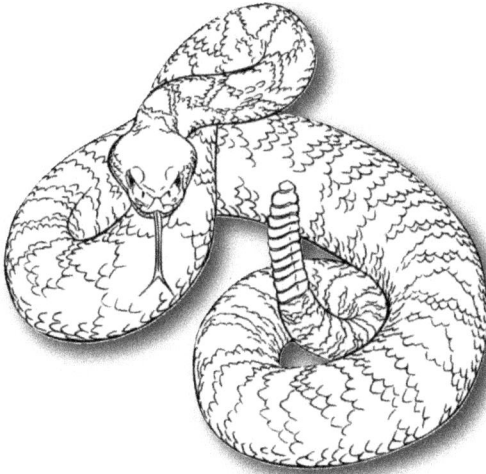

The End

Appendix

Relevant environmental organizations

Environmental Education Resource Council
Department of Natural Sciences
University of North Florida
4567 St. Johns Bluff Road, South
Jacksonville, Florida 32224-2645
(904) 620-1000

Florida Audubon Society
4500 Biscayne Blvd Suite 350
Miami, FL 33137
https://fl.audubon.org
(305) 371-6399

- *Duval Audubon Society*
  P.O. Box 16304
  Jacksonville, Florida 32245
  http://www.duvalaudubon.org

- *St. Johns County Florida Audubon Society*
  27 Fishermans Cove Rd.
  Ponte Vedra Beach, Florida 32082
  (904) 770-5484
  http://www.stjohnsaudubon.com

Florida Department of Environmental Protection
NE District Office
8800 Baymeadows Way West, Suite 100
Jacksonville, FL 32256
(904) 256-1700

Florida Federation of Garden Clubs
1400 South Denning Drive
Winter Park, Florida 32789-5662
(407) 647-7016

Florida Fish and Wildlife Conservation Commission
620 South Meridian Street
Tallahassee, Florida 32399-1600
(850) 488-4676
• *Ocala*
  https://myfwc.com

NE Florida Sierra Club
5169 Emory Circle
Jacksonville, Florida 32207
(904) 398-9482

St. Johns Riverkeeper
Jacksonville University
2800 University Boulevard
Jacksonville, Florida 32211
(904) 256-7591

The Nature Conservancy
45 West Bay Street, Suite 202
Jacksonville, Florida 32202
(904) 598-0004

Book References

1. Anderson, Robert. *Guide to Florida Wading Birds.*

2. Bell, C. Richie and Walter Kingsley Taylor. *Florida Wildflowers and Roadside Plants.*

3. Bowers, Priscilla G. *I Eat Weeds.*

4. Coile, Nancy C. *Notes on Florida: Endangered and Threatened Plants.*

5. Crockett, James Underwood and the editors of Time Life Books. *Trees.*

6. Daniels, Jaret C. *Butterfly Gardening.*

7. Fegan, Armalee, BA. *Florida's Water Resources.*

8. Peterson, Lee. *A Field Guide to Edible Wild Plants.*

9. Peterson, Roger Tory. *A Field Guide to the Birds.*

10. Taylor, Walter Kingsley. *A Guide to Florida Wildflowers.*

ABOUT THE AUTHOR

Beverly J. Fleming was the Director of the Environmental Education Resource Council of NE Florida. A self-taught naturalist, she was also an award winning photographer and writer. Her columns and articles appeared in several of the NE area newspapers.

Beverly and her husband lived on 2-1/2 acres bordering a magnificent salt marsh on the Intracoastal Waterway in St. Johns County, Florida. They landscaped their property with many native species of plants to attract area wildlife. Daily observations gave her many subjects to write about in her columns.

Her work as a St. Johns Park Naturalist, a volunteer Junior Garden Club Leader, and a public speaker helped her to educate others about the unique environment of the St. Johns River watershed area.

Beverly passed away on May 23, 2016. She was a beloved longtime resident of St. Johns County and played a key role in numerous organizations with a focus on nature. Of her many awards the one she was most proud of was the coveted Stetson Kennedy Foundation's *Fellow Man and Mother Earth Award* (2015). Her love of butterflies inspired many, young and old.